Beloved, I Love You So...

A 40 year love story told in letters

MELODY R GREEN

mrg

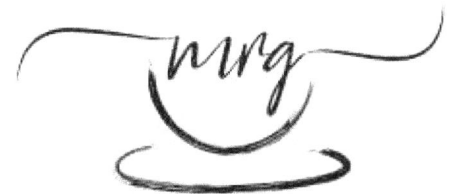

Copyright © 2022 Melody R. Green
www.melodyrgreenauthor.com
info@melodyrgreenauthor.com

Beloved, I Love You So...
Third Edition ISBN: 978-1-3937850-2-6 (paperback)
Third Edition ISBN: 979-8-2018890-9-8 (ebook)
First published by Blurb Publishing © 2016

This work is protected by copyright and all rights are reserved. Melody R. Green asserts the moral right to be identified as the author of this work.

No part of this publication may be reproduced, stored in a retrieval system, or transmitted, in any form or by any means, electronic, mechanical, photocopying, recording or otherwise, without the prior and explicit permission of the author.

No generative artificial intelligence (AI) was used in the writing of this work. The author expressly prohibits any entity from using this publication for purposes of training AI technologies to generate text, including without limitation technologies that are capable of generating works in the same style or genre as this publication. The author reserves all rights to license uses of this work for generative AI training and development of machine learning language models.

Cover Art by Jane Cornwell
www.janecornwell.co.uk
jane.cornwell.uk@gmail.com

Interior Book Design by Sarah Lemcke
www.allintheedit.com
sarah@allintheedit.com

Dedication

My Beloved,
Yesterday, today, tomorrow and always
Beloved, I love you so . . .

BELOVED, I LOVE YOU SO…

Beloved,

I've loved you such a long time.
Sometimes joyfully, sometimes resentfully, and sometimes painfully.
I've loved you in meetings, trysts, holidays, and letters.
I've loved you in times together and times apart.
I've loved you as you've travelled the globe and I've stayed put.
I've loved you in the sunshine and in the rain.
I've loved you close up and from afar.
I've loved you as a young girl and as a mature woman.
I've loved you in tears, happy and sad.
I've loved you under the sun and in the wistful night sky filled with moon and stars.
I've loved you in all of my body.
I've loved you with my mind, my heart, and of course my soul.
I've loved you even when I haven't wanted to, when I've pushed you from my heart and mind (or at least tried to).
I've loved you when I've pretended not to.
I've loved you openly, longingly, willingly, and not.
I've loved you when I thought I had no more love to give, and when I closed my heart to loving you.
I've loved you when you've travelled the world to see me and when you've gone away.
And here I am about to start my late mid-life, not yet crone and not wife . . . and still I love you.

I've stopped judging me for loving you.
I've stopped trying to figure out why or how I could.
I've stopped calling you and me names like fool.
I've stopped asking for loving you to be gone from me.
I've stopped running from all our history, real and imagined, present and not.
I've stopped trying to be with you and not . . .
I've stopped . . . I've stopped . . .
It's when you stop that magic happens.
What is . . . is.
I love you. That is all.
Dear Beloved, love is all there is between us.
Love is everything. Everything is love.
Love is all.
I accept without wishing, wanting, hoping, desiring anything.
I accept I love you, dearest Beloved.
That truly is all.
And my heart is full and deeply grateful to experience this love for you.

Beloved, I love you so . . .

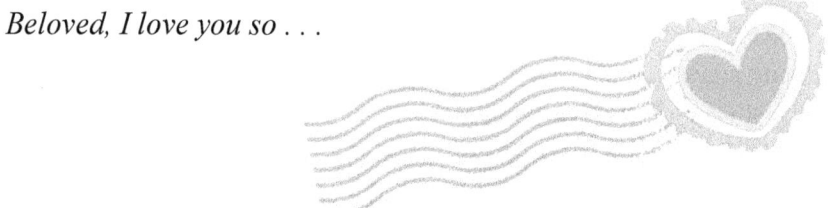

BELOVED, I LOVE YOU SO…

Beloved,

Who makes you happy, Beloved?
Who clings to you with love?
Whose arms are wrapped tight around your body, giving you a loving hug?
Who laughs at your jokes, listens to your thoughts, and feels your heart when you need them to?
Who witnesses your life and is filled with gratitude and gladness because you are in their lives?
Who makes you happy, my Beloved?
Whose eyes do you smile in?
Whose body do you make sweet passionate love to in the long night?
Who?
From the core of my heart, Beloved, I wish you these joys to fill up your life, to bring you a life you never expected or dared to dream.
Who makes you happy, my Beloved, when I cannot?
She cannot love you more than I.

Beloved, I love you so . . .

MELODY R. GREEN

Beloved,

I've often wondered . . .
What we would have shared had we spent years of our lives together? How would the fabric, thread, weft, and warp of life have joined us together?
But that was not to be for this time . . .
This time, we must have agreed to time apart to explore life apart. This time, we must have been on our own missions and adventures, taking different paths and journeys.
I didn't realize until much later that I had left a place in my heart with only your name upon it.
Once upon a time, I thought that hearts broke in pain and were left broken, but life has taught me differently. Life has taught me hearts break to allow more love in, and it's our job to leave our hearts wide open and filled with crazy paving lines and scars to show how much we have loved.
I've loved and broken my heart so much. Some scars are deeper, leaving lumpy scar tissue buried inches thick into my heart, while others are smooth, fine, and leaving barely a hair's breadth of scarring within.
I'm glad of my scars. Are you?
Did you experience them too?
Did you understand them as I have done or are they still filled with pain for you?

I hope they've healed and been replaced with lots of love.
In my special heart space where you and the memories of you dwell, there is still love.
And as a war-wounded soldier feels the ache of a battle long past, so I too ache of you. It comes in unexpected moments – a fleeting thought, a sigh, a song fragment that escapes the treasure box of my memories to remind me of you – the you I loved.
I'm glad for them, these memories. The pain has gone, yet the memories remain as warm bedfellows for wintry nights, as into the future they go and as my heart, still open, remembers you.

Beloved, I love you so . . .

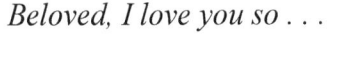

MELODY R. GREEN

Beloved,

The sight of you striding across the hotel lobby.
The sound of your voice that trembled me so . . . tugging at my laced and corseted heart as though your voice alone was the key and you the only one to speak to me of love.
The scent of you, subtle and evocative beneath the musky citrus warmth of your aftershave.
The way your collar sat beneath your jacket.
The way your mind drew maps of me, thinking, questioning, and teasing me so.
The look in eyes I could barely meet when first we met, yet could not turn away from ever since.
The heat, the spark, the electric energy of your touch.
How your fingers flicked the cigarette lighter and your hands held the steering wheel.
Your open deep laugh when I said something that delighted you.
How you always knew me . . . as if you could see through my defences and were amused by them.
How your eyes turned turquoise with desire for me.
The deep breath you took before you kissed me, as though you knew I would take your breath away.
Memories . . .
That fill me with gratitude at how you made me feel.

BELOVED, I LOVE YOU SO…

Loving you . . . I've always loved how loving you made me feel.
That was the revelation knowing you brought,
That loving you showed me how much love I could tap into and shower into the world.
Nuclear explosions of love within me . . .
Thank you, Beloved, for that gift . . .
I am so grateful, so grateful for that.
Memories now locked inside me,
Burned into the storage cells of my mind, heart, body and soul.
Beloved, my love . . . all ways, always.

Beloved, I love you so . . .

MELODY R. GREEN

Beloved,

Life is always for the best.
Even when we rail at its course.
But the way to live well at life and to succeed is to
Accept the gifts in all their wrappings, beauties, and booby traps!
Wanting what we can't have is a sure way to disappointment and despair, I've learned.
Acceptance sits inelegantly on these bones as a misshapen, ill-fitting coat might do.
No matter, Beloved, I am still yours, even now.

Beloved, I love you so . . .

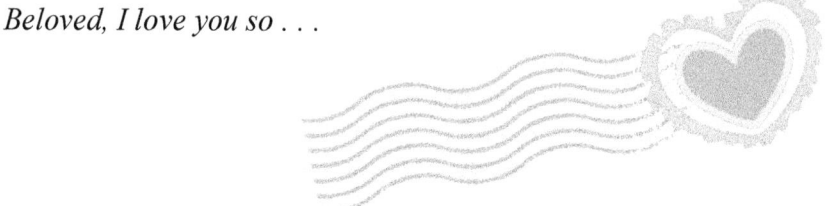

In the end, only three things matter ~
How much you loved,
How gently you lived,
How gracefully you let go of things not meant for you. ~ Buddha

Beloved,

Oh, how Buddha knew the wisdom to living a fulfilled and peaceful life!
At one time, I thought it wrong that I loved you so easily.
It is not the loving that is the issue - it is what we expect in return for the loving that gets us into trouble!
It's expecting that we should receive anything from loving.
Surely it would be so much better if we separated loving someone from wanting to be loved by that someone? We would live more gently I think. Our lives would not hold so much disappointment, pain, or bitterness.
I've discovered that with you, even though it wasn't what I wanted or expected.
I've come to understand I love you, period. And you loving me in return is not necessary to my loving you. I thought I would always carry sorrow and pain, a love unrequited if you will, but I've found it's not necessary.
I can love you without conditions of reciprocity.
This has been a marvellous discovery. It's surprisingly freeing.

It's living the love of unreturned expectations, misadventure, miscommunication, and measured or unreciprocated needs that makes love a commodity for barter.
Is love a need or a gift?
Both I think.
Love is a need which is best met by ourselves and not others. When we are free of the need for love, it allows us to release the pressure of need which sits upon ourselves and others. Then love is free, and it settles where it may.
Like a butterfly, it flits through life, touches those it chooses, and blesses us with its bounty and beauty. In that moment, it is a gift.
When love is a gift, it comes unexpectedly. We are the birds, the bees, the flowers, and the breeze, and love is the currency of life.
Love is a gift.

Beloved, I love you so . . .

Beloved,

Let us meet for a lunch of love!
And as the plates are put before us for our pleasure and delight,
Let us be fully present with each other over this simple, life sustaining repast,
Knowing it isn't the food that feeds our souls but the love all around us.
Tasting love like this is a sensual, moving pleasure . . . a feast!

Beloved, I love you so . . .

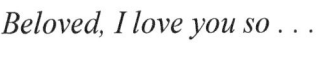

MELODY R. GREEN

Beloved,

Today I remembered the box, or should I say tin, in which your letters dwelled.

It was a very old cookie tin with a hinged lid, pressed with flowers on the top and a pattern around the sides. The tin was rusting, and the paint had mostly gone, the shine no longer present.

Of course, at the time, I didn't know about the art of Feng Shui or the power of the vibration of love or that my letters of love needed a fresh and well cared for place to help love grow. I thought only of keeping them in one place where they could be considered mementos, precious and few.

The tin makes me think of motivation . . . What was I doing? Why?

Was I confining our love by keeping it locked away? And for when, was I keeping this precious love? Was our love too precious for the light of day or the wear and tear of life?

This box of you I carried through those years with you . . . and then one day, I seemed unable to carry this love of you any further. I wrote to you, insisting you answer me immediately about where you stood . . .

I'm not sure if you couldn't answer right away or whether you deliberately gave yourself time, but the day of reckoning passed with no response from you.

I had pushed for an answer, and your silence was my reply.

BELOVED, I LOVE YOU SO…

A week or so later, I took the letters tied in their different coloured ribbons, one for each of the eleven years, and read them through, burning them in the winter flames as I finished reading them, putting the rusty old tin out with the trash. Then, when I wasn't looking, no longer expecting or daring to hope, a blue envelope arrived.

You were confused you said. You were surprised, unsettled, concerned. For you, friendship and love were still present.

I waited a few days, and then wrote what I thought would be my final letter to you.

A letter of goodbye.

One that announced a seventeen-year silence until I again took up pen and paper and regaled you with what had been happening for me, how much had changed, and yet how love remained the same.

In that time, you had settled in another country with another love.

"Are you happy?" I asked you that day on the phone.

I didn't have to see you to know your Italian shoulders shrugged. "What's happy?" you countered. Volumes spoken in those few words. You could never hide your heart from me.

"I'm settled," you said. You had settled for what you had, what was easiest, the life you'd built.

"I have you in my heart," you said, "And that is all I dare do. To do more might be wonderful, but it could also be terrible. I don't have your courage. I never really did! You were always the bright star, out of my league."

Again I let you go. Again.

There were no losers here and no victors, for love simply is . . . and fear also.

For that brief moment, all time was present, all love was here, there was only now.

But love in the now needs both parties to accept love's power. One cannot hold it for the other, and so I let go as the next moment moved onward.

Time passes as sand, and love too cannot be contained or grasped . . . only felt and let go.

MELODY R. GREEN

These days you come fleetingly on zephyr's breeze, the power of the jinn in the evening's darkness whispering insistently . . .
"Do you remember me? Am I forgotten? Do you love me still?"
And I, unnerved in that moment of surprise, say,
"Of course, my Beloved! You are my heart's heart, the core of my Soul, my flame of existence.
You are love, and I love you still!"

Beloved, I love you so . . .

Goodbyes are only for those who love with their eyes,
Because for those who love with their heart and soul
There is no such thing as separation. ~ Rumi

Beloved,

Finally, I came across the writings of Rumi and Hafiz, and it was as though someone had finally spoken from my heart and given my soul the words to express itself.

Of all the reasons I have come here to earth this time, there is no doubt within me that expressing my heart's love in creative form is one of them.

At the publication of my first book of poems, a reviewer spoke of my profundity in the simple, my philosophical expression of love, and the way I see love in everything.

Maybe I am like Rumi and Hafiz. I see love as the light that leads us through the mundane. My poetry is written in essence not verses. It is distilled in moments of love.

Love is expressed in moments over time, yet each moment is complete unto itself.

This I feel is the core of me.

This I know love to be.

And love flows from me as a river.

Some come with a bucket to know love. Others will come with a thimble.

MELODY R. GREEN

No matter. All will feel filled with love.

Beloved, I love you so . . .

Beloved,

When I say I miss you, I mean . . .
Everything reminds me of you, and so I see you everywhere.
When I say I miss you, I mean . . .
I wonder about you and me . . . I wonder if the promises in your eyes and lips still glow brightly for me or have they been spent... Are they forever gone?
When I say I miss you, I mean . . .
I talk to you often for you are all around me. You hang in the ethers of love. Each particle of love contains you.
Sometimes I conjure you into consciousness, but mostly you come unannounced, surprising me with your visit.
When I say I miss you, I mean . . .
I gaze into the still moments of staring nothingness, and I know you are there. Sometimes as palpable as a touch, at other times barely perceptible in the mists of nothingness.
When I say I miss you, I mean . . .
I imagine you . . . what are you doing in all this space away from me? How are you feeling? What joys and sorrows visited you today? Always, are you happy? Oh, I so wish you to be happy!
When I say I miss you, I mean . . .
I look forward to a moment when we meet anew. Knowing this may be in another dimension other than earth. So be it.
When I say I miss you, I mean . . .

MELODY R. GREEN

I think of all the ways I've yet to grow and hope you are growing too. I feel sure growing and blooming is one of our plans on earth, My Beloved. I hope you do too.
When I say I miss you, I mean . . .
I sometimes regret . . . like poison it runs through my veins where once they ran with love for you. Mostly I regret my fears that I followed. Thinking if I loved you the way I truly felt, in the way I wanted, that you would run from me in fear yourself.
These days I love you, period. Love is.
When I say I miss you, I mean . . .
I remember as though the moments we shared were only a moment ago rather than years.
When I say I miss you, I mean . . .
I resolve to love from the inside out and into the world fully, no fear, no doubt, no second guessing. Loving outwardly in the now. No waiting for the right person, right place, right time to love.
Love cannot be held back. Love must be free to be expressed.
When I say I miss you, I mean . . .
I long to tell you of all I've learned by loving you and letting you go. I do miss you, but I miss the way loving you made me feel so alive, delighted, and happy with you . . .
Yes! I miss the aliveness to love, to you, to me, to us, that loving you gave me.
I miss you.

Beloved, I love you so . . .

Beloved,

When it was time for me to come to Earth, I sat with my advisors to decide what this life would be like. . .
"Will my Beloved be on Earth this time, and will I meet him?" I asked.
"Yes, he is and, yes, you will meet him."
"Good, I'll go." I jumped up, ready and willing to go to Earth.
Now I see that maybe I should have asked some other questions that might have revealed more of how our meeting would go and what to expect. But the excitement of seeing you in earthly form and feeling the love for you in this third dimension of time, space, and matter was too strong an impulse.
Love is like that. And so I came, we met, and my life this time has never been the same.
From a soul perspective, any opportunity to express love with a soul mate is worth everything to experience. So it is with you.

Beloved, I love you so . . .

Beloved,

Life has taught me . . .
Choosing to give love is always better than withholding yourself for fear of being hurt.
Life has taught me . . .
Being afraid of love only hurts me, not the other.
Life has taught me . . .
Withholding love makes you ill.
Life has taught me . . .
Love desires to love full out wherever it may be.
Life has taught me . . .
Love is not subject to conditions. If conditions appear, it is not love.
Life has taught me . . .
Love is always free. If it is not free, it is not love.
Life has taught me . . .
Love is always a choice we make – sometimes we don't remember when and where we made the choice!
Life has taught me . . .
Love never needs an introduction.
Life has taught me . . .
Love is always about expanding into more love. If love is less or if there is contraction, it's not love.

BELOVED, I LOVE YOU SO…

Life has taught me . . .

Beloved, I love you so . . .

MELODY R. GREEN

Beloved, my kiss will tell you all I cannot say. ~ Melody R. Green

Beloved,

So many different kisses I had with you . . .
Shy, gentle, barely there kisses.
Hot, heated, be mine now kisses.
Reverent, so precious is our love kisses.
Quick, capture the fun of now kisses.
Fleeting, maybe I'll see how I feel kisses.
Hello, my God, you're here kisses.
Soft, exploring sensual kisses.
I love you, but I'm afraid to tell you kisses.
I love you, can you feel how much kisses.
I'm afraid of love kisses.
What a joy, you love me kisses.
Exploding fireworks, light behind my eyes kisses.
I wonder if I'm kissing you kisses.
If I kiss you, will you kiss me back or run away kisses.
Are you real kisses?
Passionate, lazy, lust-drenched kisses.
I am yours, you are mine kisses.
Whisper I love you kisses.
Soft, ethereal, remember me kisses.
I delight in loving you kisses.
How lovely kissing you is kisses.

Kiss me, I am yours kisses.
Kiss me now, demanding kisses.
Sad, poignant, soon you'll be gone kisses
Help, wait…please don't go, kisses.
Surrender, surrender, I am undone kisses.
Amazingly you are mine kisses.
Oh, what a surprise loving you is kisses.
I'm in heavenly bliss kisses.
You are so amazing, I can barely believe it kisses.
I'm crying deep inside kisses.
What will I do without you kisses?
You're going, and I'm hurt kisses.
Sealed with a loving kiss letter kisses.
Oh, you've written to me, how wonderful to hear from you kisses.
I can't bear us parting kisses.
I can't believe you're promising me the world kisses.
Can this be true kisses?
You've hurt me more than I can say kisses.
Oh, I hurt kisses.
Kiss my tears away kisses.
Soul filled kisses.
Sweet chocolatey kisses.
Wine filled kisses.
Quick, before they get here kisses.
Hidden in the dark kisses.
Hold me close because you can kisses.
Stolen in the night kisses.
Dawn rising parting kisses.
I'll be back soon kisses.
I promise . . . kisses.
Don't be afraid kisses.
Please, please, don't go kisses.
Last goodbye, oh, this hurts kisses.
Pulling apart goodbye kisses.

MELODY R. GREEN

Not here, I'm overwhelmed kisses.
Peck kisses because I'm scared to show you how I really feel deep inside kisses.
Long, succulent love kisses.
I've never tasted anything as good as you kisses.
You are my life kisses.
Breath of life kisses.
Nibbling, playful kisses.
I'm hungry for you kisses.
Oh Beloved, so many different kisses I've had with you.

Beloved, I love you so . . .

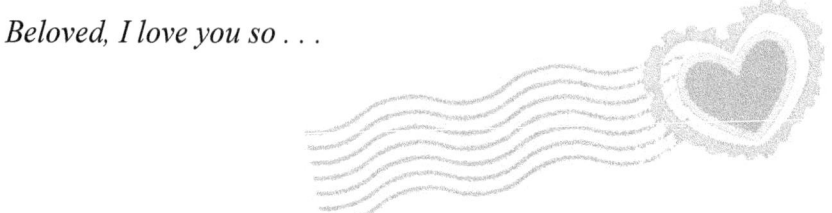

*Love is a journey into the unknown.
Trusting it is why we are here.* ~ Melody R. Green

Beloved,

Isn't it strange that we forget that we are love and go searching for it as though it were some lost sheep in the wilderness?
And isn't it stranger still that we forget we are love and believe it is something so completely outside our self as to be separate from us?
Searching, always searching and then, when found, we are suspicious of its place in our life. We worry if we are safe with love. We become addicted and neurotic with love, questioning the love we've found.
For those of us who yearned for love and felt unloved in our early childhood, there are added pains and neuroses to overcome. If we felt unloved, then we need to find out what love is. How love can flow in our lives and how to trust its presence. Life as a result is full of false starts, unsure middles, and heart-wrenching ends.
But all of it's for growth!
An unloved child does not become a healthy, loving, and loved woman or man without some serious experiences along the way. And for real love to be found, the ability to love oneself without the input of others to find the truth – that we are all love – love needs for us to be alone, contemplative, and seeking the hidden within.
Without realizing, this is what I chose. To learn to love me, not to feel my worth according to others. Loving others was the easy part. Loving

myself was where I needed courage. I turned within. I turned my back on the old, and then I could concentrate on learning to love me, to heal the broken parts of me. Ironically, this is not as selfish or self-indulgent as it might seem. I think it is an act of loving others too. For when you love yourself, the capacity to love others grows exponentially.

Of course, loving others doesn't give them what they want all the time, in the same way as loving yourself doesn't.

But it does mean you are suitably comfortable in your own skin, psyche, and soul to give your lovers the space to be them as well as giving that to yourself.

Loving oneself allows for loving another more authentically, truthfully, and lovingly.

It is the inner journey with love that is the journey with the unknown, and it is this journey that requires absolute trust.

How are you with your journey now, my Beloved?

Beloved, I love you so . . .

BELOVED, I LOVE YOU SO…

Beloved,

We are moving into the month of February, and here I am wondering why we have all this fuss on St. Valentine's Day?

I can see the very clear materialism of the day. The advent of greeting cards brought the day to more prominence in the nineteenth century, but that was in a time when writing letters was important. It seems less so now in our electronic world, and yet I was brought up in the time of letter writing.

I love writing letters. It is a ritual I indulge in. I love the scratch of the fountain pen against the smooth skin of the paper, and I miss the way greeting cards are becoming less important. I've always loved receiving letters and cards, maybe because I was a migrant kid, a stranger in a new land wanting desperately to belong, and letters helped with that belonging.

I never expected us to write. I'm not sure why I went to the trouble of connecting with you. After all, at that point I could have said, "No! He's gone, let's move on. Even with the feelings present."

I suppose I have my years at boarding school to thank for my letter-writing skills and habits. We were made to write letters home every week, and I got into the habit of it.

Even with my family and the cheapness of phone calls, I would still put pen to paper, even if it were a dashed off note.

But my letters to you were different. These were not dashed off. There was always a ritual to them. To the table I would bring your previous letters to reflect on, a cup of tea to lubricate the prose, my fountain pen (and, if I remembered, the ink), onion skin airmail paper that allowed me to write more than an aerogramme, and an airmail envelope, usually blue.

I wrote in all weathers and times of the day, but my preferred time was Sunday in the afternoons before supper.
Although if I had had a busy day rehearsing, it might be after supper. Writing the letter was only part of the exercise.
There was also time needed to reflect, recollect, and recount my life to you.

In between my letters, cards. Always cards at St. Valentine's Day and of course the time to allow it to be delivered. For me, St. Valentine's Day was always late January to ensure it would arrive on time wherever in the world you were.
Sometimes, letters and cards together. Sometimes, photos, reviews, or the odd newspaper cutting from my life.
Paper is such a fragile material on which to record a life of love, don't you think? Our precious moments and feelings held together by ink on paper. The historian in me was totally comfortable with that. I had read many letters from famous men and women to their sweethearts. Surely I was in excellent company?

Maybe if I had kept a diary, I would have written less. Who knows? But there we were, one letter leading to another. A chain of love stretching forward over eleven years. So much time of turbulence for us – deaths, pains, tribulations, but successes and celebrations too. Our lives intermingling like breaths and, with each line scribbled, love as a vine took over and grew. Delicate threads woven between our souls in patterns of love that had travelled many lifetimes before and who knows how many lifetimes into the future. I suspect this love is not over, no matter how it may look in this lifetime.

BELOVED, I LOVE YOU SO...

Love, it always comes down to love. No matter if we accept it, embrace it, deny it, or reject it. Love exists outside of us and our whims.

Thank God! Imagine how much worse the world would be without the persistent determination of love in our lives! It doesn't bear thinking about, does it, Beloved?

Beloved, I love you so . . .

MELODY R. GREEN

Beloved,

You are my dearest one.
When I think of you, my heart opens and softens
And, as though my heart were a pot of succulent, fragrant casserole,
I remove the lid, and the perfume of love bursts forth,
Filling the space with love aromas.
Your name is enough.
The thought of you, the heat from the fire and love escapes me.
As though you have sat at the table and eaten the meal, I assume it flows to you.
And I, like the pot, know where the stew of love has been.
Fragmented flavours stick sweetly to me to show that love has been here and done its fill.
Love, always love erupts from me. Love works, so much "saucery" in my being at the thought of you.
You are the Beloved, my dearest.

Beloved, I love you so . . .

Beloved,

You speak in many languages. Yet I remember you most in the language of love. So fulsome, nuanced this love language, travelling the world in its many tongues.
I've learned some of them and been seduced by others.
But you, my Beloved, spoke a love I never heard before or from anyone but you.
This is the magic of love . . .
It's unique to those willing to express it!

Beloved, I love you so . . .

Beloved,

I loved receiving your letters. Do you know why?
I loved the lines filled with the idiosyncrasies of English being not your first language.
Of course you were fluent, yet every now and then a verb juxtaposition would give you away . . . and then the words on the paper would be living sounds, and I could hear them as words from your lips.
And then there was your lettered hand. The way the words filled the page, the shape of your love words, the calligraphy of you.
From the first moment I saw the first letter, your name and address measured on the back of the envelope, my name written by you.
Oh, such joy at the sight of it! I never tired of receiving your words.
My hand in comparison reflects so much the speed of my thoughts and feelings. With each word changeable and erratic, where as your hand flowed across the paper in bold, measured, and generous lines.
I have found I am very sensitive to a man's hands. It was one of the things I disliked in my partner you know. His handwriting was tight and small. I wish I'd taken notice of that before I found myself saying yes to him. It might have made me question who he really was, for of course he was like his writing. His pocket was held tightly to him, and his mind was full of small ideas that felt overwhelmed by my spirit and wished to always close me down. But I overcame all that smallness, control, and tightness, and I bloomed into me finally.

BELOVED, I LOVE YOU SO...

While love is in our heart, we will always have the energy to bloom, no matter how long it takes us to do so.

I've watched and spoken to many late bloomers, and I'm always amazed at how small the amount of energy is required to catapult them forward into their true selves . . .

The love . . . they are meant to be.

Beloved, I love you so . . .

MELODY R. GREEN

Beloved,

Now I have decided fully to write to you, to release the feelings and thoughts I have accumulated in the last years without you . . . I am amazed at how much love for you has lain dormant within me.
I don't know if these letters will ever see the light of day or if they will remain as a diary of my love thoughts for you.
For the moment, I don't care.
I am simply being with my thoughts, trying to express love that has lain deep within me. I realize if I don't explain myself, you will think I've held love for you and denied myself and others the beauty of love, but this is not the case.
Love has always been within me in great abundance it seems. Always waiting for the opportunity to spring forth like a song that was a constant low hum and then at appropriate moments burst forth into the rich choral sounds of love.
If I look at the love I came with as part of my DNA, I have always had more love than my English heritage could comfortably allow. I was love unreserved, emotion oozing out of every pore, refusing confinement and spilling over all the edges.
My first contact with foreigners where arms and bodies gesticulated emotions both grand and small, filling the space with their vibrant, musical juiciness, was a revelation to me and such a joy. At last, I thought, there are others like me. I am not some weird throwback, a one-off reject. For look! They're rolling their emotional lives out like

some magical carpet that shines brightly with coloured sparkles and noisy exclamations!

Here was warmth, excitability, and aliveness. In my own culture, I was being suffocated, my spirit crushed almost into extinction.

But this brief memory, savoured and hidden away when I was nearly nine years old, surfaced again in my late teens and, like a genie escaping a bottle, once released could not return. I met others from all walks of life and rejoiced in their differences and all they could teach me about love.

And now I remember a moment, many years later, when I realized that even grouping love types together in nationalities, regions, and villages was still too restrictive.

For the Source of All is so much more variable than that.

Love, the Source of All, is unique in each and every single expression of itself on our glorious, abundant Earth.

I stopped wanting to travel like the gypsy I had become and instead longed for settling and allowing myself to meet the love travellers along my way who would express themselves beautifully, just the way they were.

I am not yet settled though, not deeply rooted in the world, and yet I feel this is most acutely needed now.

As this letter shows, love is a traveller who meanders where love may. All we can do is dance with love when it shows up and not worry when it appears to leave.

Beloved, I love you so . . .

MELODY R. GREEN

Beloved,

I am an apprentice at love. All my life has been about learning what love is . . . experiencing its many flavours and attributes and all the emotions that love spawns.

Love is a master of giving us the life we need, not necessarily the life we want. I only have to see how love has shown itself in my life and within our relationship.

This is what I believe happens . . .

We arrive on Earth filled with love and, as we watch our primary carers show us their love lives, we create beliefs according to what we see. To this we add fairy tales, marketing campaigns, love days and holidays, written materials, movies, and music lyrics so that, by the time we reach puberty, we are already programmed for love in ways that may have nothing to do with who we are or what as a soul we may want to experience in our lives.

And then we add sex to the mix of love, romantic love, hormones, social mores, conditioning, and religious programming, and we are in many ways doomed not to find real love until many decades later. Possibly when we've loved and lost many times, been married and divorced and become parents. It is rare to find anyone unscathed by this.

If we are brave, we move through this minefield of love, and who we are changes positively. We are honed by love into greater understanding and a larger capacity that enables us to recover from the pain of love, move into the acceptance of the vagaries of love, and finally revel in it.

I feel I've completed my apprenticeship of the modules of love called Love and Pain, Love Unrequited, and Love Disappointed.

I have learned a lot about love in passionate creation. I adore creative expression and want to do so much – it has been a great love.

I have loved as a mother. Without doubt my greatest achievement and the one that has brought the most fulfilment. It took me a while to appreciate this love but, once realized, it was a delightful experience to be my son's mother and, even now, when he is a young man of twenty four, I am still delighted in him in so many ways. It was such a privilege to be asked by him to be his mother. He clearly brings out the best in me.

Yet relationships with men have not always seemed to bring out the best in me. Instead, my insecurities, neediness, jealousy, paranoia, lack of confidence and self-esteem have reared their heads. Relationships with men have worked in my feminine shadow, bringing forth what needed to be healed. They showed me where I was out of love with myself, and this understanding eventually moved me into greater self-love. My lesson I feel has been to love myself in a healthy way, thereby enabling me to love others that way too.

Which I suppose leads me to you.

These days I love you so much better than I did in my youth. I love you for you. All you are, have been, and are yet to become. I do not love you because I want something from you, and my love is not measured in love returned. . .

I'm smiling here . . . Love does that to you.

Beloved, I love you so . . .

Beloved,

St. Valentine's Day . . .
Love on one day?
Nooooo!
Love in every moment, every day?
Yessss!
Loving you is an all time, all day, every breath of life, affair.
Let others have their St. Valentine's Day.
I prefer to love you with every breath of love in my being.
My Beloved, you are my every-thing.

Beloved, I love you so . . .

BELOVED, I LOVE YOU SO…

Beloved,

It always amazes me how I can fall deeper in the love that is you . . . being you.
It amazes me especially when falling and heights disturb me so. Why is that do you think?
Deeper and deeper in love with you.
Another magic place love takes us, my Beloved one.
Is this why we follow love so ardently – to follow the magic?

Beloved, I love you so . . .

Beloved,

Recently, after another foray into love that tore me asunder,
I had an epiphany.
I need to give myself all the love notes I've written for others and so I address them to me.
Some of them are here.
I wrote them on pieces of different coloured notepaper and put them in a pretty box. When I'm feeling fragile in the loving me department (as we all are want to be at some time in our lives), I pull out a few of the love notes and read them aloud. It's surprisingly therapeutic, and my heart that might be feeling vulnerable at being alone remembers I am all one, and the tilt of my lance goes into balance, and the world is righted again.

I so love you my goddess, my love, my delight!
You are the grace I hoped for in my life, you are love, my Beloved.
I am surprised at how often I look at you and my heart goes warm and mushy with love and tenderness for you.
I love how you laugh, my darling!
I am in awe at all you do. There is such magic and love in you, my darling.
Your smile is gentle when you look at me. Thank you.
You are the colours of my rainbow, my love.

BELOVED, I LOVE YOU SO…

When you look at me and smile, I'm blinded by the light of your love . . . thank you.
Your world should be bright with the stars of the universe.
You are such a blessing!
You are my love goddess.
Only with you can I truly know love.
You are the brightest star in my universe.
I am so blessed to love you.
Be tender with me, my darling, I love you.
You are my waking thought and my day's companion, my love.
There are no words today to express how much I love you.
Please accept this kiss from me, Beloved, it's filled with love for you.
When I sleep, I dream of you, still feel your presence, and know you are love.
I am so blessed loving you.
I have been transformed utterly. At a cellular level. Loving you has done this to me.
Loving you is such a joy to me – can you feel that?
If you left me, my world would be loveless, lifeless, drained of all that is beautiful. This is how important your love is to me.
When I feel alone or afraid, sad or blue, I remember you.
The love of all I survey, the love of all I am, and I breathe in your love, so grateful I have you.
How did I get so lucky to be with you, I wonder?
You, Beloved, are my angel love.
You make me happy, happy, happy . . . I love you, Beloved.
I love watching you sleep. It makes me love you more.
I really, really, really, truly, truly, absolutely love you, my darling.
Please forgive me. I forgot for a moment how precious loving you is.
I love when you're silly!
I love that you are the age you are and yet still a kid!
Love words, sweetheart, remind me of how precious you are to me. I love you.
Love, you are everything, my every-thing!

MELODY R. GREEN

I'm so smitten by you.
You love me unstintingly – I am so blessed.
I love you more than love itself. Bowing low, my goddess.
Bowing low in gratitude, love, and pure bliss.
You are love present. You are love's present.
You are love, how can I not love you?
Darling you! You are the one I love. Now. And. Forever.
I am overwhelmed by how much I love you, my darling.
Sweetheart, what need do I have of sweetmeats and treats when I have you, my darling heart?
Hot pink and delicious! Yes, this is you, my darling one.
I am breathlessly in love with you, my darling.
I love how I am when loving you, my sweetest heart.
I am blessed. Bliss filled, loving you, my darling heart.
Love is . . . your breath as you sleep. I love you.
You are my music, my colour, my world. I love you my sweetheart, I love you!
Beloved goddess, I adore you. You've opened me to love, joy and happiness I've never known. How could I not love you?
Sadness has gone, joy's arrived. You are here, my sweetheart.
You make my day and night for you are here, my darling one.
What joy you bring me, my darling!
Thank you, Beloved. I am deeply grateful for your sweet love.

Beloved, I love you so . . .

BELOVED, I LOVE YOU SO...

If you knew yourself for even one moment
If you could just glimpse your most beautiful face
Maybe you wouldn't slumber so deeply in that house of clay
Why not move into your house of joy and shine in every crevice
For you are the secret treasure bearer – and always have been
Didn't you know? ~ Rumi

Beloved,

Rumi - he always knows how to say it best.
My words always seem to fall short of his glorious essential clarity. But still I try. I let his poetry fill my heart, mind, and being and then try to write of how I love you.
Maybe it is the limitations of English or rather I should say my limitations of it. Other languages of love have sweeter sounds than mine.
I remember when we migrated to New Zealand. It was the first time I had heard Dutch, German, French, and Italian.
Of course I was only nine, so I suppose it would have a great impact on me. I was in the passageway near our cabin when I heard Italian for the very first time. I remember the sound as though it were only a few moments ago. I don't know what the cabin crew were saying. It didn't matter really. I just remember the impact on my skin . . . as though the membrane of my skin had turned to a swimming pool of water and the words broke the surface, diving deeply in, vibrating and

bending waves throughout the pool. The sound stopped me, and I held my breath, waiting in excited anticipation until the next sound became a current running through my body. The sound of Italian in my ears and on my skin changing me forever.

Was it any wonder Italy, Italians, their music, art, and culture would be so important to my life?

Beloved, I love you so . . .

BELOVED, I LOVE YOU SO…

Beloved, loving you is such a pleasure. ~ Melody R. Green

Beloved,

Love is a pleasure, no matter its flavours, textures, and colours.
Loving you has given me the chance to explore love.
A small, secret smile plays along the curve of my older lips, and my eyes soften in focus and drift off to another time and place where you and I are locked . . . a memory cell of my soul's being.
There was a time when this would have been impossible to do, especially when I dwelled in the pain of not being with you. But time soothes those moments and love, always present in all ways, remembers and brings forth the sweetness.
It's then that pleasure rises, and love can be appreciated for what it is, an ever-present delight. The pearls joined together into a love strand of jewellery, a sign of our lives being filled with the glorious moments of love.

Beloved, I love you so . . .

MELODY R. GREEN

It is not that love limits you
It is that you limit the fullness of love. ~ Melody R. Green

Beloved,

Today's truth I think.
Maybe we are all afraid to feel the fullness of love. I know I have been. Because we are afraid of love, we splinter love into fragments and say "I can only love these ones. I can't be too greedy. It's wrong to take from others. Others deserve love more than me."
We believe love is measured and in lack. I've never believed that love is limited, but I have believed I don't deserve it, that I haven't been beautiful, talented, or worthy enough for the love I've seen others have. I've thought myself to be a fraud, soon to be exposed. This constant expectation that I will be revealed as an imposter and have love taken from me kept me anxious around love.
I wasn't a fraud to love or others. I was a fraud to myself. I robbed myself of love and short-changed my love bank at regular intervals.
But no more. I don't do this anymore, but I did in the early days.
I'm glad our paths crossed this time on our journey through love on Earth. It was wonderful to meet you this time, my love.

Beloved, I love you so . . .

Beloved,

Here I am with my morning coffee, held in my two hands, steamy aroma rising from the rim. I so love the smell of coffee, and it so reminds me of you.

Why is that do you think?

After all, it's not like you introduced me to coffee. I drank it before you, and I've drunk it since.

Maybe it's the way you drank it. Espresso, stirred quickly with two heaped spoons of sugar and then tossed to the back of your throat in one single shot. Coffee shot home to start your motors running.

When I think of your hometown, Roma, I imagine you stopping at one of the many café bars on your way to the office. You in your business environment, a line of men waiting for their caffeine hit. Baristas lined across the narrow bar that is filled with steaming café machines and the aroma of beans, roasted, ground, and cooked through vapours rising and falling, permeating the other aromas of testosterone, cologne, perfectly groomed football crazy, *la dolce vita* living Italian men. Yes, I know it's a cliché, but cultures and national identities are filled with those, aren't they?

They can be untrue though, I remember your surprise one evening when you commented, "My English Rose, you surprise me with your Italian heart!"

MELODY R. GREEN

Most of us wear masks to fit in and hide the truth of who we really are. That's why we are so intoxicated by love. It gives us a chance to unveil ourselves, even if it is only in the inner sanctum of love's boudoir.
The warmth of my coffee cup has cooled as the memories mingle with the coffee vapours and float away. The sun rises, promising another beautiful day. Time to move forward into what today brings.
Thank you for the simple yet delicious memories of you.

Beloved, I love you so . . .

Beloved,

It has been a while since my last letter but don't dare to think you've been out of my thoughts. Rather, you have been entwined in my everyday thoughts. Flitting easily and gracefully in and out of my days, reminding me that life is but a string of pearls, each pearl a moment of beauty.

Fleeting, momentary, and gone so quickly. Isn't it a shame we are consumed by the mind's insistence to create something permanent our egos can hold on to when really there is only impermanence all around us?

Our hearts know better. Feelings are eternal and timeless. I am convinced that all life is about is living our emotions out loud. Unfortunately, it's taken many years of suppressing my feelings and my heart under the smooth mask of control. It took illness for me to understand this.

My body, heart, mind, and soul experienced a schism that left me in dark places. It's easy to fall into this place if I'm not aware. I'm grateful for the awareness and the rawness of life.

We can't escape our darkness. We must learn to journey through the terrain, looking for the signposts to return to the light, and then be so very grateful we've arrived in the bright daze of a sunlight vista.

MELODY R. GREEN

Life is like that, filled with light and shadows. Love is present in both for we are love exploring love in both.

Beloved, I love you so . . .

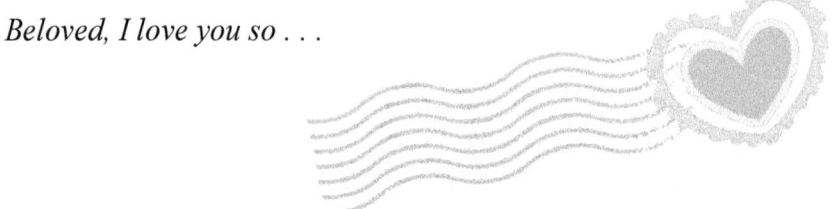

BELOVED, I LOVE YOU SO...

Beloved,

Here I am sitting in a café, watching the world go by, surrounded by humanity living out life, and I smile as love catches my eye.

Across the road, a man and a woman start the first of the courting rituals. They are smiling, flirting, being love present, and as I watch them exchange love, a smile crosses my lips and a twinkle fills my eye. For yes, I remember as though it were only yesterday our banter, exchange, smiles, teases, breathless exchanges of pleasure, leaning in, slight touches . . .

My heart softens with memory.

It was wonderful wasn't it, darling – those heady days of first meeting . . .

I'm so glad I had those moments with you.

Beloved, I love you so . . .

Beloved,

I've been thinking about how we live our lives. When I was young, I wanted to live my life as a grand adventure, do you remember?
I wanted to conquer the world, claim it as mine, and make my mark! I threw myself at life as though I was indestructible. From these words, it might appear as though I were an adrenaline-fuelled extreme sport junkie but no, nothing could be further from the truth. No, my world to conquer was the emotions – mine and others. My world was about expressing the emotions, helping others feel them, and to see what a world would look like if it was fuelled by love.
Back then, I didn't understand this emotional landscape. I didn't comprehend the fragility of our minds, the resilient strength of our hearts, or how our souls will keep pushing us to experience life to the fullest. Our hearts and minds are the last frontier. Until we understand, we will continue to assault, abuse, and act in anger against ourselves and others, and the world will be filled with the bodies of broken humanity. When we are in pain, we cannot see clearly the pain we inflict on others and nature around us.
We stop inflicting pain on others when we learn about our own pain and heal it.

BELOVED, I LOVE YOU SO...

You taught me to let our love shine through the cracks of pain so we can grow stronger and bigger and allow more love in, not less. Thank you for the lesson.

Beloved, I love you so . . .

MELODY R. GREEN

Beloved,

Let me love you as you are,
With your strong oppositions,
Your weak thoughts,
Your stubborn resistances,
Your shields, your barriers, and castle drawbridges.

Let me love you as you are,
With your frailties and your fears,
Your boogie man in the darkest night,
Your sense of yourself not quite true,
Your nearly perfect holy masculine strength.

Let me love you as you are,
With doubts the size of monster marbles,
As emotions like flying fish in a small fishbowl
Climb your insides.

Let me love you as you are,
When you are spent of all that's good in you,
When you've poured yourself with all the love you have in you
Into the sacred cup in the hope you'll find paradise.

Let me love you as you are,
When your victory cries silence the tree birds,

BELOVED, I LOVE YOU SO…

And the sun blinks at your shouts of joy and happiness,
At your unbeatable odds success.

Let me love you as you are,
When you come forth and beg me to dance with you,
And the moon and stars fill the world with soul light,
Echoing the song within us
To show us we are not alone.

Let me love you as you are . . .
Beloved one.

Beloved, I love you so . . .

MELODY R. GREEN

Beloved,

I'm amazed at how frequently you pass through the sieve of my mind and remind me you are always with me.

I can be doing something as simple as washing the dishes or folding the laundry, and there you are! Standing behind me, whispering in my ear in that laughing way you have that lets me know you're teasing me again. And as soon as I register your presence, it is as though your arms are around me in a loving hug.

Sometimes the hug can last many minutes, and it is so real as to make indents on my skin, and I feel your breath against my ear. At other times, it seems only fleeting, and then you're gone.

This is what assures me that those we love are with us always, even if they've moved on to others or passed to spirit, no longer here on Earth. Love is love and always present within us and around us if we but bother to take the time to slow down, still our busy minds, and be. Because I know you can be here at any time across dimensions, I can feel when you are present and yet not feel lonely.

And that, my dearest one, is a wonderful thing.

Beloved, I love you so . . .

Beloved,

As much as you return to me and I can feel your presence, I can in the next moment forget completely that you exist!

I remember in the early days of having this sensitivity to your visits that I always felt guilty when I forgot you. Now I think I understand more clearly. We need to move our presence from one moment to another, and in each moment, we can choose to have vast sensitive extending awareness or be only present to what is most pressing in this now.

Living at heart is an extended awareness of what are past, present, and future moments all at once, but it can stress our systems. It takes practice in the same way learning to be an Olympic swimmer might stress muscles, tendons, sinews, and bones. It takes effort, but practice makes it easier.

If I need you, I can call you. Not that I do this as I am aware you are living your life without me, and it's important for me not to interfere. Should I at any time decide to be with another love, then my auric doors would be closed to you, and you would not be welcome to visit as you do now. When both of us leave this earthly plane, I'm sure we will be able to catch up, share our adventures, and carry on as the love we are.

But for the moment we are here.

MELODY R. GREEN

I am grateful I can connect with you as we do.

Beloved, I love you so . . .

Beloved,

I miss you in strange moments when I least expect to . . .
Sometimes when I am at the coffee shop, the smell of coffee will make me think of you.
When I see beautiful leather handbags in that gorgeous tan lustred leather.
When I see a man using a man bag.
When I see gelato pinks, icy pale blues, and pale limoncello colours, I think of you.
When I see beautiful clothing in a man's clothing shop.
Silk ties, cuff links, linen handkerchiefs, cashmere sweaters, and linen jackets.
A certain alchemy of male cologne that assaults my nose in wafting sensual notes. First the cool freshness of lime and other citruses, then a green note of bay flooding my nose and head, expanding my lungs, and finally, setting my heart afire, the warmth of ambergris and woods. The aromas of cologne undo me, and my nose twitches in search of the elusive perfume of you mixed with those other sophisticated ones. All my cells push forward to capture you, but of course you are not there. My olfactory cells shrink, deflate, and close at not finding you, and I feel heavy with disappointment.
In these moments, I need to rebalance into my own perfumes, and I sniff my wrists to find where my perfume sits, breathing in deeply until I can centre myself within me.

MELODY R. GREEN

Sometimes the sound of a doorbell that I may hear in a film or on television, the exact timbre and tone of the doorbell you rang all those years ago, will remind me of you. For many years, I got physically sick when my doorbell sounded. So much so that I had to disconnect it and only reconnected it when it was time to leave and let someone else hear you arrive at the door.
And of course, there is always the music that I associate with you – your music, my music and, where they entwined, our music.
Love is built on many moments and facets of sensual bliss as love opens our senses as much as it opens our hearts.
And while I can hear the tone and timbre of your voice and would recognize you in a crowd of fifty men and my chest would expand, my heart beat a tattoo and my blood sing at the sound of you in my veins, it is my sense of taste I cannot, dare not remember.
In my cave of memories, there is a unique volume all about you – the sacred and the unforgettable tastes of our love, of you, and of the foods we shared.
Maybe when I am ready to pass and I need to bring forth the memory, I will dare to open this volume, but until then it must stay closed, or I might lose my sanity or whatever it is that keeps me moving forward into the life of my tomorrows.
Through my senses, I know I love you with every fibre of my being, dearest one.

Beloved, I love you so . . .

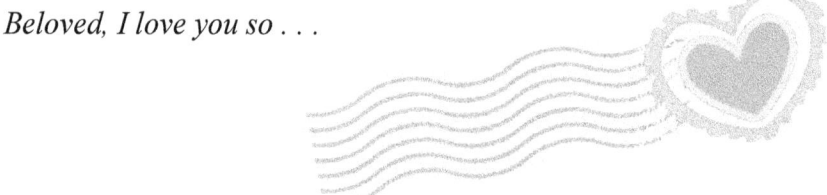

Happy Birthday, Beloved!

Beloved,

Another year passes, and again it's your birthday - how can they travel so fast? I remember a similar conversation with you at my 21st birthday. Do you remember, I wonder?

Do you remember I remembered your birthday every year we were together and apart? So much care and love went into those gifts for you. Hours of looking for just the right thing – cuff links, tie pins, monogrammed handkerchiefs, writing implements, desk toys, and silver-framed photos.

Things I hoped you would treasure and cherish. Did you? Do you still have them? Or use them? Do they help you remember me? Or are they gone to the ethers of time, my gifts passed on to others or given to charity shops? I would love to think they are with you, but my practical self says they've probably gone, like so many things from your past, for that is the way of the world we live in, isn't it?

Today is your birthday, and you are celebrating your seventieth year. Seven decades of time on this planet Earth. I hope you are able to look back with love, joy, and pride in all your life has been and be filled with thanks for the wonderful experiences you've had, the people you have loved, the lives you've changed, and all those who've changed you and helped you grow. Life is short and swift, a blink of the eye, and you're gone. From stardust you came, and to stardust you will go, Beloved. Meet you in the stars!

Beloved, I love you so . . .

Beloved,

I'm sad. Today I lost another good friend to cancer.
She was feisty and a fighter. She loved her children. She fought for better conditions and a better world.
She was a colleague in arms. She spread her passions across her world. She loved others better than she loved herself.
And she died too young . . . far too young.
And I'm angry . . . She left me before I had finished being her friend . . . What am I to do with all I had to give her that she did not claim? Where do you store that love, that laughter, those experiences aborted before their time?
It's as though I have a painting half-finished where her thoughts, laughter, and love were to go. I'm holding on to the painting for fear I will forget her . . . that she will be taken over by the insistent pull of life that marches inexorably on.
So, I have decided to paint our half-finished friendship and put it on my wall. That way I will not forget her, and when the time has come to move forward to the other realms, I shall take that painting, meet my friend, and say, "Let's continue where we left off, weaving love and laughter into each other's lives." And she, in her no-nonsense way, will laugh at my whimsy but be secretly glad she had my friendship, my loyalty, and my love for the long days we were apart.
In fact, I suspect she is here now, laughing at my silliness.

MELODY R. GREEN

Today I lost another good friend to cancer, and life moves inexorably on . . . and she is gone, like some part of my being seems lost but is not.
There will be a time under heaven when all that seems lost is found, and so that shall be for us, my Beloved.
And across the space of time know . . .

Beloved, I love you so . . .

Beloved,

I didn't realize you'd invited me to lunch!
I thought I was sitting here in the café at the botanical gardens in early spring simply enjoying the day. It's an outdoor café. My coffee sits untouched, and I feel your presence . . . such a delight! And to show that love is present in all things, I am also visited by a beautiful dragonfly. He sits on my newspaper so I can admire his beauty. Yes! No doubt he is your insect counterpart. You so loved to be admired. You pretended otherwise, but I knew you loved the attention of all the beautiful women who wanted to be a part of your life.

They wanted your arm to preen possessively upon, wanted your attention, your love, the glint of humour in your blue eyes. Yes, you knew those blue eyes, your fair hair, and height drew the ladies like bees to the honey pot. You were like a precious truffle. Women sniffed you out and paid exceeding homage.

I knew it from the first, and so I insulted you instead.

Maybe some part of me both wishing to stand out from the crowd and be remembered, and another part of me not wanting to become one of those women. I was young and did not understand my allure. I never realized the power of my gaze, nor the stillness and depth that attracted men. I had to have others tell me that. Those who recognized it and wanted the secret wisdom of love and life they saw in my gaze.

But I was like the other women, in awe of you. I cooed and ahh-ed at you, feeding you with my adoration.

MELODY R. GREEN

I'd like to think I would be more blasé now, but something tells me I would be just the same. Taken in by the magnificence of you.
I watch the dragonfly sitting gracefully on the newspaper, his wings shimmering with light as he senses the breeze.
With a slight flick of his tail, he rises and moves up on the breeze to another who will love and admire him. He's had enough of my love. I wish I could say the same for me.

Beloved, I love you so . . .

Beloved,

In all seasons I love you.
But it is the damp blister of late autumn, the earth still smouldering from the heat of summer that I love you best.
Autumn makes me grateful for the warmth of you to lean on as the cold wind whips our heels. To wander the comparative warmth of the museum on the hill and then, wrapped loosely in each other's arms, to settle into the warmth of home cooking, warming soup, and toasted chunks of ciabatta.
Bliss.

Beloved, I love you so . . .

Beloved,

Love has taught me to be grateful for moments, all of them. The good, bad, ugly, exquisite, indifferent, caring, boring, exciting, anxious, blissful, drab, colourful, loud, quiet, sweet, sour, bitter, salty, dry, and succulent.
They are all wonderful if we can but let out hearts see and feel them fully.
Love moments are like the jewelled colours of a stained-glass window. Individual pieces mean nothing much alone but placed together create the most glorious design of love and life.
Thank you for being part of my window. . .

Beloved, I love you so . . .

Beloved,

I've been feeling this but putting it off. Wanting to linger but also knowing it's time. When I started writing these letters this year, I didn't know I was trying to finally say goodbye, but indeed this is what I've been doing.

Today I made a paper tissue flower with a petal for every letter I've written. All the colours of the rainbow I adore, faintly coloured, diaphanous, finery. All that our love was and is.

You might ask why goodbye?

It is time for my heart to expand and grow further than it has ever done. My heart angel housekeepers are clearing my heart space. Spring cleaning it for the new. Painting the walls with hope and openness. Putting in new curtains of joyfulness and refurnishing the space with happiness.

Our hearts came in this way, but life tends to betray our sweetness and trust. We become clogged with old hurts, hard feelings, and sad stories. It is time for me to renew my heart to its ever-present glory. It is time to be open to life's journey, to be open to love's business. Farewell, my Beloved, until we meet again, as surely, we will. For we are from the stars, and to the stars we shall return, brighter and more sparkling than when we came here, for we have played with life and love and returned to tell the tale.

Now and always Beloved, I love you so . . .

MELODY R. GREEN

Acknowledgements

Memoirs are funny things... because of course there are so many people that make your life the way it twists and turns, but in this case especially "G", he knows who he is... thank you for the opportunity to learn so much about love.

And my friends who've put up with me over the years, and may have heard parts of this story many times. (Big smiles!)

And especially my Spirit guides, who have helped me understand and find peace after a lifetime of turbulence - you guys need a medal for your patience and unconditional love!

On a practical note:
When I start writing a book, I create a book cover for it. It's a psychological thing, it helps me focus. So I sent this to Jane Cornwell and she came back with the finished product efficiently and with excellent ideas to make it polished and attractive.

I am so pleased to have come across the work of my editor and interior book designer, Sarah Lemcke at All in the Edit. Nothing was too much trouble.

And to you dear reader. My hope is you'll read this story and remember your own love affairs with affectionate acceptance for all the many delights they gave you.

As the Angels say...Love is all there is.

Blessings

About the Author

MELODY R. GREEN

Melody R. Green is an Angel Intuitive who uses her gifts to help people work through the ups and downs of love, relationships, and the other big events of life, guiding them to connect back to "Spirit" and their own intuition. She has much first-hand knowledge of connection to Spirit as she lives in her in a home filled with spirits of many kinds, who speak to her often. Melody lives in Armidale, NSW, Australia.

CONTACT DETAILS
Website: www.melodyrgreenauthor.com
Email: reviewers@melodyrgreenauthor.com
Instagram: www.instagram.com/melodyrgreenauthor/
LinkedIn: www.linkedin.com/in/melodygreen/
Facebook: www.facebook.com/melodyrgreenbooks

Also By
MELODY R. GREEN

Maggie McCready's Travelling Tarot Adventures

BOOK 1: THE ANGEL TEA HOUSE

BOOK 2: THE PILGRIMS' WAY CAFE

BOOK 3: THE PENDRAGON TEAROOMS

MAGGIE McCREADY OMNIBUS

WISH BOMBS, BAKING SPELLS AND RECIPES

A Tipsy Man Goes Naked:
Love Tales and Recipes

Beloved, I Love You So

The Art of Flirting
and Seduction

Also By
MELODY R. GREEN

Maggie McCready's Travelling Tarot Adventures

THE ANGEL TEA HOUSE

BOOK 1

Maggie McCready is a travelling tarot reader who offers spiritual advice over a cup of tea and a charmed biscuit or two.

Maggie arrives in Angel Street to support tea blender and café owner, Lucy Silverton who is being targeted by unknown sectors of the community, undermining her confidence and business. Maggie must find out who is bullying the businesses of Angel St Business Network while keeping herself safe. This is her first mission assisting Archangel Michael and the Legions of Light to protect the suburb from the encroaching dark forces. Armed for the fight with only her kind heart, tarot deck in hand and her entourage of mystic beings, she has a lot to learn about Spirit, the dark forces and herself before this adventure ends.

Something is brewing in Angel St, and it's not just the tea!

Also By
MELODY R. GREEN

Maggie McCready's Travelling Tarot Adventures

THE PILGRIMS' WAY CAFE

BOOK 2

Maggie finds herself in an adventure with eight Archangels (including Archangel Michael) who have asked her to help them clear the negative energies around a very old pilgrims' route on Dartmoor, called The Archangels' Way. They're on a mission to rid the Way of the impact of human history, smugglers, highwaymen, ghosts, pixies, energy centres, churches, ley-lines, death, peat bogs, gallows, haunted inns, rolling mists, stone circles, standing stones and holy wells.

It's a fascinating place with energy wormholes and crossing points between the dimensions giving Maggie and the Archangels plenty of disturbances to try to balance and of course Phineas, Archdemon and the Archangel of Chaos is there to make the task as difficult as possible.

Also By
MELODY R. GREEN

Maggie McCready's Travelling Tarot Adventures

THE PENDRAGON TEAROOMS

BOOK 3

Maggie finds herself travelling to Stonehenge and Glastonbury at the request of Pendragon, Dragon High King of Britannia, to help him save the Dragon Queen of Avalon from the encroaching dark forces.

But Maggie is without her usual ally, Archangel Michael and finds herself at the crossroads between Spirit and the nefarious mundane realm of drug and sex trafficking.

To add to her discomfort she is romantically pursued by the not quite "honourable" Mac. How will she reconcile her need to work for the light with her love of a shadowy Scottish biker?

And where is Archangel Michael, when she needs him? Even Archdemon Phineas, the Archangel of Chaos seems to have disappeared. It's all rather odd and Maggie feels as though she's floundering on her own in this summer adventure.

Also By
MELODY R. GREEN

Maggie McCready's Travelling Tarot Adventures

THE OMNIBUS

Meet Maggie McCready, a travelling tarot reader who offers spiritual advice over a cup of tea and a charmed biscuit or two.

The Omnibus edition brings together all 3 of Maggie's adventures that will whisk you away into a world where mysticism and danger intertwine.

Book 1 - The Angel Tea House

In the heart of Angel Street, a mystery brews stronger than any tea. When dark forces stir, only a tarot reader can read the signs. Something is definitely brewing on Angel St, and it's not just the tea!

Book 2 - The Pilgrims' Way Cafe

In the heart of The Archangels' Way, a mystery brews stronger than any tea. Mystic paths, ancient spirits, and one tarot reader's courage shine through on a supernatural quest to cleanse the haunted pathways of Dartmoor's storied pilgrim route. Step onto The Archangels' Way with Maggie and her celestial allies to find out more.

Book 3 - The Pendragon Tea Rooms

When the call of destiny leads Maggie to the heart of Britannia's mystical sites, she must face both supernatural and earthly dangers to protect the sacred balance. The lines are blurred between good and evil, will Maggie's tarot wisdom be enough to guide her through the darkness?

Also By
MELODY R. GREEN

Maggie McCready's Travelling Tarot Adventures

WISH BOMBS, BAKING SPELLS AND RECIPES

Maggie McCready is a travelling tarot reader who offers spiritual advice over a cup of tea and a charmed biscuit or two.

In this book Melody R. Green answers the many letters from readers wanting the recipes, baking spells and wish bombs Maggie used to bring some magic into the lives of those she met in The Angel Tea House, The Pilgrims' Way Cafe and The Pendragon Tea Rooms.

Inside you'll find:
* Detailed instructions on how to make wish bombs and how to combine essences and herbs for bath and shower bombs.
* Spells and incantations to protect loved ones, heal a broken heart, or find a new job, or home.
* And a variety of recipes for sweet and savoury treats.

Author Melody R. Green has compiled all of Maggie's secret spells, enchantments, and recipes into one bewitching book! Wish Bombs, Baking Spells and Recipes has everything you need to bring a little bit of magic into your life.

Also By
MELODY R. GREEN

A Tipsy Man Goes Naked

Join the mysterious "Muse of Aroma and Taste" as he presents a tantalizing collection of short stories, mouth-watering recipes, and enchanting anecdotes in a single day from breakfast to supper.

You'll embark on a culinary adventure across the globe and through the ages as the Muse intertwines fairy tales and heartfelt narratives of love.

Through the art of cooking and storytelling, he challenges readers to ponder the complexities of love: its endurance, its various forms, and its ability to heal. As you flip through the pages, explore the depths of emotion, flavor, and touch as he serves up a delectable feast of sensual delights for your heart and soul.

This modern day collection is reminiscent of the Tales of 1001 nights and Scheherazade and a glorious celebration of life, love and food.

Experience the harmonious fusion of romance, gastronomy, and introspection in this evocative blend of storytelling and culinary artistry, where each chapter serves as a gateway to a realm where love blossoms in all its forms.

Also By
MELODY R. GREEN

The Art of Flirting and Seduction

Have you ever wondered why some men and women can charm the birds from the trees while others can't?
Or why flirting and pick up lines sound so right with one person but false and cheesy if used by another?
It's all to do with authenticity.

In The Art of Flirting and Seduction, Melody R. Green explains what to look for and how you can increase your flirting and seduction quotient by being aware of the philosophy and mechanics behind giving pleasure to others by what you say and how you say it.

If you are looking to find the best one-liners to chat up a man or woman this book is NOT for you. But if you are wanting to learn the attributes and mindset of a flirter or seducer then you've come to the right place!

In this tongue in cheek look at flirters, seducers and stayers Melody R Green takes us into the laws of engagement, the art of flirting, serious seduction and even commitment and goodbyes.

The flavour is light and playful, the information thought provoking. Practice makes perfect... let's begin!